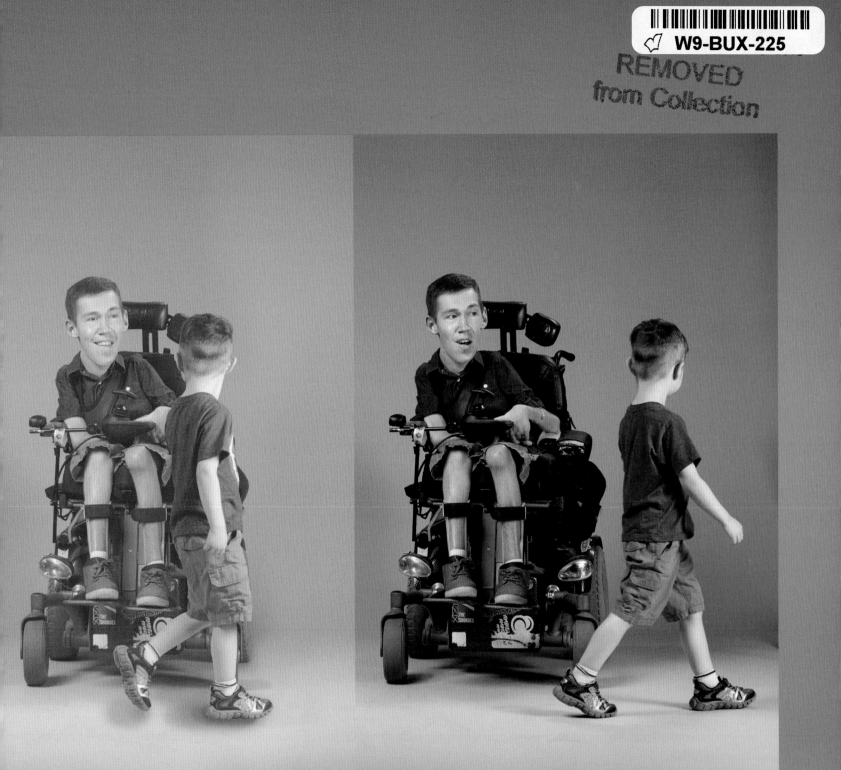

Not So

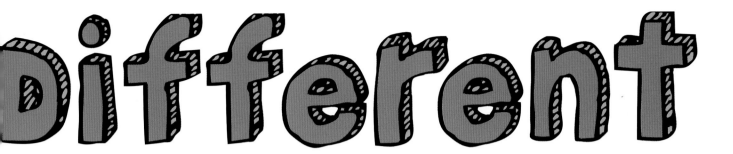

Different

What You REALLY Want to Ask About Having a Disability

by Shane Burcaw

With photographs by Matt Carr

ROARING BROOK PRESS/*New York*

To my coworkers at LAMN, Erinn and Sarah,
for working with me to make a difference
—S.B.

To Shane for making the difference
—M.C.

With special thanks to Ben Mattlin and my wonderful editor
Claire Dorsett for their valuable feedback
—S.B.

Text copyright © 2017 by Shane Burcaw
Photographs copyright © 2017 by Matt Carr
Published by Roaring Brook Press
Roaring Brook Press is a division of Holtzbrinck Publishing Holdings Limited Partnership
175 Fifth Avenue, New York, NY 10010
mackids.com

Library of Congress Cataloging-in-Publication Data

Names: Burcaw, Shane. | Carr, Matt, 1971–
Title: Not so different : what you really want to ask about being disabled
  / Shane Burcaw ; photographs by Matt Carr.
Description: New York : Roaring Brook Press, [2017] | Audience: Age 6–9.
Identifiers: LCCN 2016058267 | ISBN 9781626727717 (hardcover)
Subjects: LCSH: Burcaw, Shane—Health—Juvenile literature. | Spinal muscular
  atrophy—Patients—United States—Biography—Juvenile literature. | People
  with disabilities—United States—Juvenile literature. | Neuromuscular
  diseases—Juvenile literature.
Classification: LCC RC935.A8 B8725 2017 | DDC 362.4/3092 [B]—dc23
LC record available at https://lccn.loc.gov/2016058267

Our books may be purchased in bulk for promotional, educational, or business use.
Please contact your local bookseller or the Macmillan Corporate and Premium
Sales Department at (800) 221-7945 ext. 5442 or by e-mail at
MacmillanSpecialMarkets@macmillan.com.

First edition 2017
Printed in China by Toppan Leefung Printing Ltd., Dongguan City, Guangdong Province

1 3 5 7 9 10 8 6 4 2

Hi!

My name is Shane Burcaw. I bet you have some questions for me. Many people do! They stare and wonder all sorts of things, so I want to answer their most common questions, and yours, head-on.

What's wrong with you?

Playing in the sand with Mom in
Emerald Isle, North Carolina

Getting my legs stretched out in my stander

Pretending to drive Dad's truck

Absolutely nothing is *wrong* with me. I'm just a little different!
I was born with a disease called spinal muscular atrophy, or SMA
for short, that makes my muscles very weak. It affects all the
muscles that help me move—my arms, legs, neck, and more. I've
been like this since I was a cute little baby.

Watching TV with my brother, Andrew

My childhood best friends, Ben and Harry, and my brother, Andrew

My body doesn't have the proteins that it needs to create new muscle, so I can't get stronger by going to the gym and working out. Scientists are working on a lot of different possibilities to treat my disease, but so far they haven't found one that works.

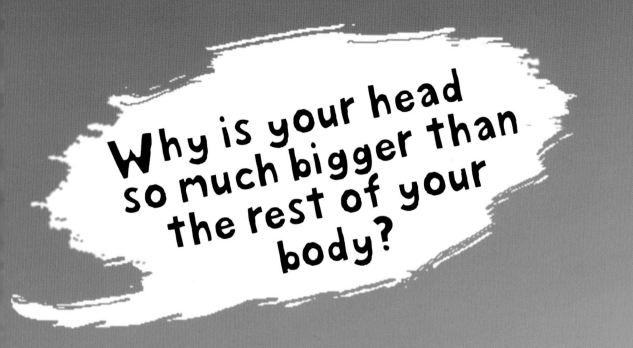

Why is your head so much bigger than the rest of your body?

I've never been able to walk, and since my disease is progressive, I get weaker as I get older, meaning that my arms are weaker now than when I was a kid.

Because my muscles don't grow normally, my body has stayed pretty small. But my head and my enormous brain were not affected by my disease, so they grew to a normal size. I admit it might look a little funny sitting on top of my tiny body.

Don't let it get you down, Shane. My head is big and my arms are short too, but I'm still awesome!

But how do you do things?

I need help with a lot of things. Luckily, I have great friends and an amazing family. This is my mom, my dad, and my brother, Andrew.

No one else in my family has SMA—it's actually very rare and affects only about 1 in every 10,000 babies. But even though they don't have the disease themselves, my family still lives with it every day by helping me.

Almost everything!

They help me shower using a special bathtub chair. Then my dad helps me get dressed and my mom helps me comb my hair so I look handsome.

My brother helps me brush my teeth, but he loves to joke around, so I don't let him help me get dressed or he makes me wear ridiculous outfits.

They lift me into bed every night when it's time to go to sleep, and help me roll over in the middle of the night when I'm uncomfortable, too.

They also help me go to the bathroom by lifting me onto the toilet. I have a special seat with a strap on it so I don't fall off— or in.

How do you eat?

I love eating! It's one of my favorite things to do, but since the muscles in my mouth are very weak, I try to stick with softer foods, like mashed potatoes, mac and cheese, and pizza. Sometimes I eat them all at once. My family helps me by cutting my food up for me.

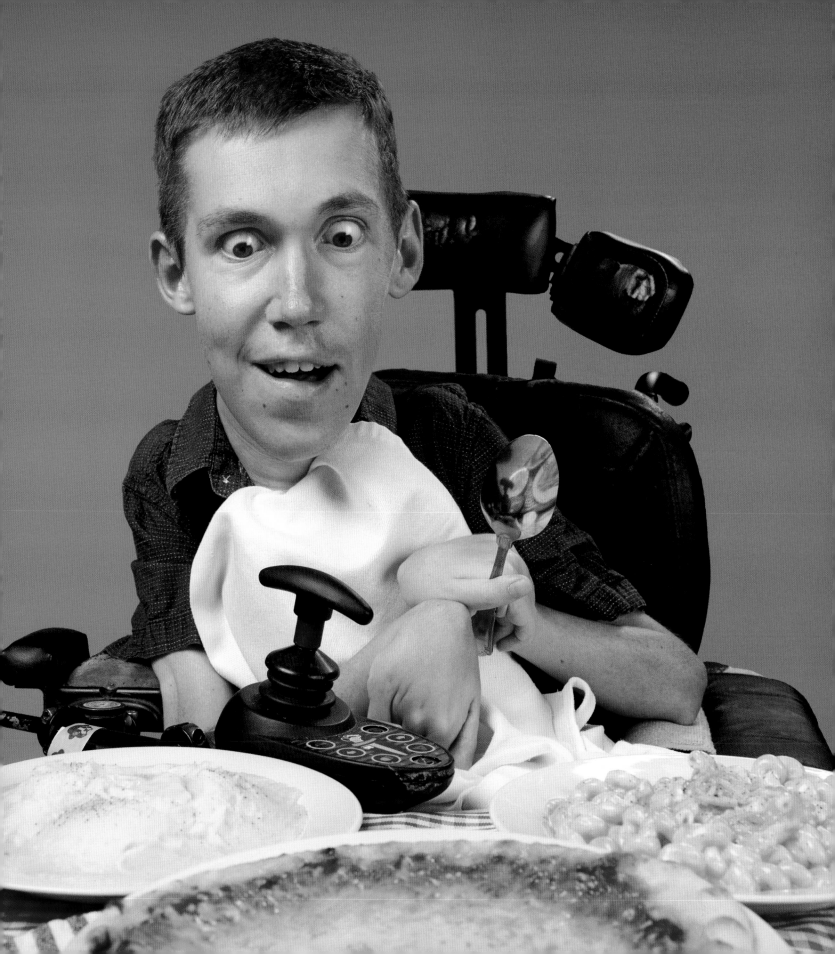

HOW does your chair work?

HANDLEBARS —————

SNACK COMPARTMENT —————

ROCKET BOOSTERS—————

SAFETY LIGHTS

Although I get a lot of help from my family, I am able to do a lot of things myself too, because I have this awesome motorized wheelchair that helps me move around. I drive it using a joystick, sort of like a video-game controller. I get a new chair about every seven years, and my doctors help me pick out the model that best suits my needs.

BACKFLIP PREVENTERS

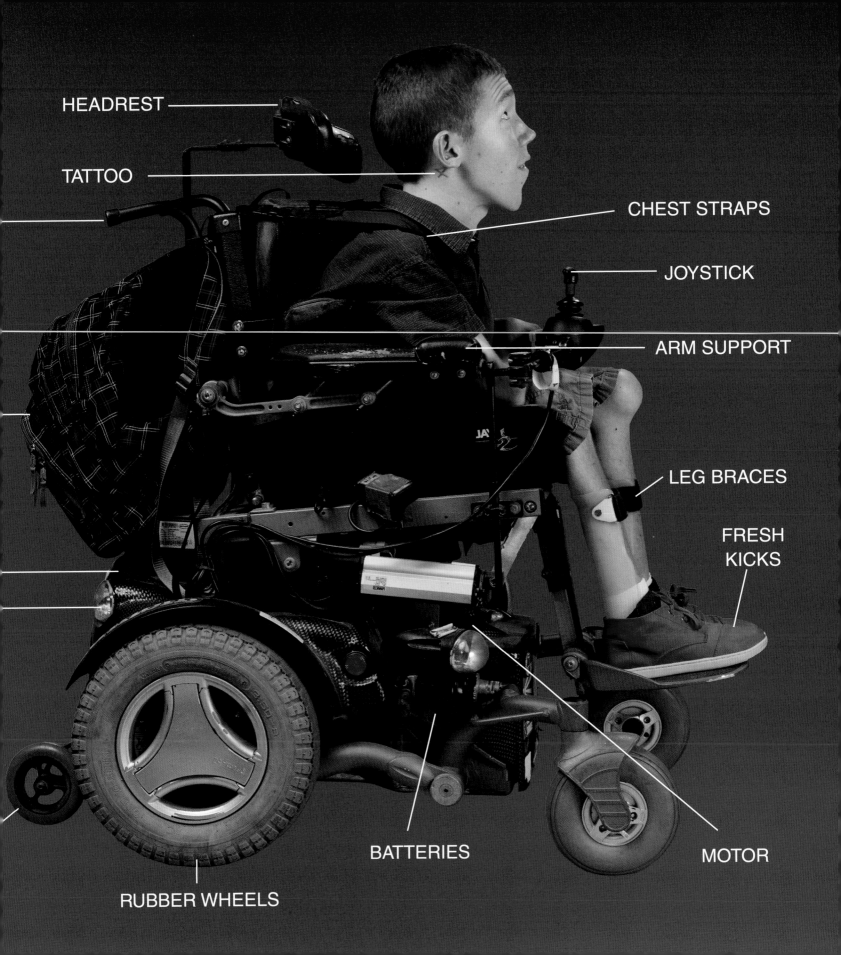

HEADREST

TATTOO

CHEST STRAPS

JOYSTICK

ARM SUPPORT

LEG BRACES

FRESH KICKS

BATTERIES

MOTOR

RUBBER WHEELS

I can drive my chair about as fast as you can ride your bike, and I wear safety straps to make sure I don't fall out.

I can pop a wheelie with my brother's help!

And I can even drive it in the snow—but it's very slippery so I have to drive carefully or I'll crash.

Once, I tried to pull my brother to the top of the basketball hoop with a rope tied to my chair. But that broke my chair's motor, which was very expensive to replace.

My wheelchair costs more than a brand new car, and since it is so important to me, I try my hardest to take very good care of it. Please ask me before you touch it!

Can you
climb
stairs?

Stairs are impossible,
but luckily many places
are wheelchair accessible.
I can use ramps instead
where they're available,
and I have an elevator in
my room that helps me
get to the basement.

The
Shane-O-vator

I have a specially equipped van that I get into using a ramp. Once I'm inside, my family or friends help strap my chair to the van's floor so it stays stable when we drive. Although I don't drive myself since my arms are so weak, I still love going on road trips with friends!

How do you play with your friends?

My friends and I do a lot of the same things together that you like to do. We play video games, go to the beach, and hang out and talk. We also love to make each other laugh.

We love to play sports together too. We have to find different ways to play so that I can participate using my wheelchair, but we always make it work. For example, when we play football, instead of tackling people, I just run them over.

When we play soccer, I am able to hit the ball with the wheels of my chair. But I have to be careful too! One time when I was playing soccer, I forgot to put my safety straps on and I flipped out of my chair onto my head. Ouch!

Occasionally, and it hurts my feelings because if they knew me a little better, they would see that I'm not so different!

I believe it's very important not to judge a book by its cover, so when you meet someone who looks different from you, it's always best to treat them with kindness and respect.

After all, that person may end up becoming one of your best friends.

I love making new friends, so if you see me out and about, don't be afraid to come up and say hello!

AUTHOR'S NOTE

Spinal muscular atrophy—commonly abbreviated SMA—is a rare neuromuscular disease under the wider umbrella of muscular dystrophy diseases. That's always a mouthful to spit out when people ask, so I like to explain that the disease, which I inherited from my parents who both carry a recessive gene for it, makes my muscles waste away as I get older. Our bodies have two basic proteins used for creating and sustaining muscle, and I'm lacking one of them.

There are four basic "types" of SMA, which vary in severity from the most severe (Type 1) to least severe (Type 4). For a long time, Type 1 SMA was the leading genetic cause of infant death in the United States, but advances in medical technology have extended that life expectancy greatly.

I was born with Type 2, meaning the condition wasn't noticeable until I was about nine months old. I never developed the strength to crawl or walk. Now, as I'm getting older, things like swallowing, breathing, and arm movement are being affected as my muscles continue to deteriorate.

The more than thirty forms of muscular dystrophy are broadly characterized by progressive muscle weakness and the deterioration of skeletal muscles that assist with movement. The disorders vary in terms of severity, progression, inheritance, and the type of weakness caused. There are no cures, but medical breakthroughs have been robust lately, and many treatments are finally coming to fruition.

My disease has had an enormous impact on my life, but I try not to let it define me. I am, above everything else, a writer. Sharing my humor and my perspective through writing is my biggest passion. My first book was a memoir called . . . you guessed it, *Laughing at My Nightmare*. It shares all the ups and downs of my ridiculous life for the first twenty or so years.

Beyond that, I'm a sports freak. I love watching soccer and football and baseball, attending live games with my friends when I can. I also love traveling, which isn't always the easiest for someone with my condition, but with the awesome companionship of my brother and my girlfriend, I've gotten to see more of the world than I ever thought possible.

Speaking of my brother, my family is a huge part of my life. They are my primary caregivers, and it's tough not to be close with the people wiping my butt every night. Am I allowed to say that in a kid's book? I even cofounded a nonprofit, Laughing At My Nightmare, Inc. (LAMN) with my cousin, Sarah Yunusov. The two of us were attending college together in 2011 as my blog (the original source of the name), began to rise in popularity. As my readers climbed into the hundreds of thousands, the two of us realized there was an opportunity to help people with the simple idea of laughing at our adversities.

Today, LAMN is my full-time career. Our company provides two essential services. We travel the country performing speaking engagements to kids and adults alike about the "power of positivity," teaching people how changing our cognitions can help us live better lives. We've spoken to over eighty audiences in two years, and we both agree that the experience has been nothing short of life-changing.

We also fund-raise like crazy—the more traditional function of a nonprofit, if you will—so that we can provide vital equipment grants to individuals living with muscular dystrophy. We added this facet to our mission about two years ago, and we've already provided upward of $40,000 in grants to more than twenty-five individuals across the country. We provide items that make life more healthy, comfortable, and productive, from ramps and van conversions to medical devices and adaptive technology. You can learn more about our mission at laughingatmynightmare.com.

Through my writing and my nonprofit, I'm working tirelessly to help children develop a better understanding of disability. So many of the social stigmas that people with disabilities face could be squashed if we were able to instill in young people the idea that we are all different; we all have different strengths, weaknesses, and abilities, and that's not just okay, it's beautiful. I hope that this book accomplishes that in some small way.

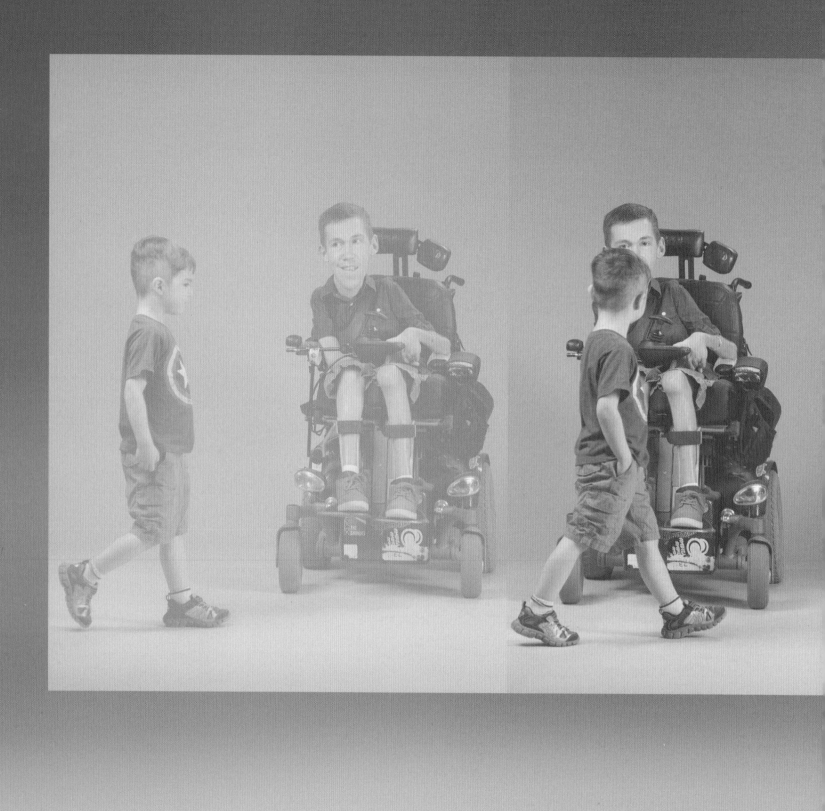